THE TEN COMMANDMENTS OF GOLF ETIQUETTE

How to Make the Game More Enjoyable for Yourself and for Everyone Else on the Course

By Roland Merullo

Illustrations by John Recco

"This terrific book, by a wonderful writer and a pretty fair golfer himself, is not just for beginners. It will demystify golf's sometimes bizarre etiquette for anyone who loves to play, and surely make the game more fun for all."

—Bob Carney , Contributing Editor, *Golf Digest*

"Golf, a magnificent addiction for the initiated, can be a mystery for newcomers hoping to pick it up. Roland Merullo's *The Ten Commandments of Golf Etiquette* is the Rosetta Stone for anyone looking to break through the game's clutter of rules and protocols. It combines Merullo's passion for golf with his gift for clear writing, humor and insight. *The Ten Commandments of Golf Etiquette* brings the first tee a little bit closer—and makes it a lot less daunting."

—Tim Murphy, retired Senior Editor, *Golf World*.

The Ten Commandments of Golf Etiquette:
How to Make the Game More Enjoyable for Yourself and for Everyone Else on the Course

By Roland Merullo

Illustrations by John Recco

PFP, INC

publisher@pfppublishing.com

144 Tenney Street

Georgetown, MA 01833

April 2015

Printed in the United States of America

First PFP edition © 2015

ISBN-10: 0990889831

ISBN-13: 978-0-9908898-3-0

This book's suggestions on safety issues are only that—suggestions. Golf can be dangerous. Please use good judgment when you play, and follow the rules of common sense and the safety recommendations at each course or driving range.

TABLE OF CONTENTS

ONE

THOU SHALT BE QUIET

In just about every other sport it's okay to yell, cheer, heckle and harass at any point in the action. In golf it is not. Part of what makes golf such a unique and wonderful game is the respect players show for each other—at all levels. In keeping with this tradition, try to always be aware of the other people in your group, and the others on the course. When someone is ready to hit, don't talk, cough, sniffle, clear your throat, blow your nose, sigh, talk on the phone, check your messages, text, whistle, or tap your driver against your shoe. If at all possible, don't move.

It's perfectly okay to cheer or applaud if someone in your group makes a great shot or sinks a long putt, but remember: on a nearby hole there might be a player who's standing over a key putt or about to tee off. That person doesn't want to hear you scream:"GREAT

1

SHOT MIKE!" in the middle of his or her backswing.
When you are swinging or putting, you'll appreciate the
courteous quiet of those around you.

TWO

THOU SHALT BE SAFE

Although it's not a contact sport, golf can be dangerous. Every year thousands of people get hurt playing the game, and you even hear about golfers who are killed on the course. Almost all these injuries are preventable if you follow certain basic guidelines.

You should never stand in front of someone who is hitting, and never stand so close behind him that you're within range of the widest arc of his swing. On the fairway, always let the person farthest from the hole hit first, and don't stand in front of him or her, even if you're at an angle and twenty yards away. Beginners, especially, have been known to hit the ball sideways, even at a 90 degree angle sideways.

Before you take a practice swing, especially on the tee, be absolutely sure that the other players see you and are standing a safe distance away.

Remember, a hard-hit golf ball can ricochet off a tree or stone wall at amazing speed and unpredictable angles. If someone behind you or on another hole yells "FORE!" don't look up! Cover your head or the back of your neck and turn away.

If there's a tree or a boulder right in front of you, don't risk taking a full swing at your ball—chip out sideways.

If your ball lies on or near a tree root, it's often better to move it and take the penalty rather than try to hit it and risk injury to hands, wrists, elbows, or shoulders.

Always watch the person who's hitting, and never, under any circumstances, hit at the same time as another player in your group.

Wait for the group in front of you to be a safe distance away before you swing. If in doubt, give them another minute to walk or drive farther forward. And if you hit an errant shot into a different fairway or close to another group, don't hesitate to yell "FORE!" as loudly as you can and as soon as you see where your ball is headed. And then go over and apologize as you're walking toward your ball. A simple and sincere "Sorry, I should have waited," or "Sorry, I didn't think I could reach you," or "Sorry, I didn't see you there," will do. If another player offers you a gracious apology like that, graciously accept it. We all make mistakes.

Even after the group ahead of you has finished putting out, you should wait until they move a safe distance away from the green area before hitting.

In certain parts of the world, if you hit into the rough or near a water hazard, keep your eyes open for snakes, alligators, crocodiles and other creatures that might think they have more right to the territory than you do. Bees, chiggers, ticks, ground hornets, wild boar, rabid coyotes—none of these will be sympathetic to you in your search for a mis-hit ball.

On some courses the holes run parallel to each other and are separated only by a thin line of trees. On courses like that, always be aware that a golfer on the next hole can hit an errant shot into your fairway, and might not see you, or might see you and neglect to yell "fore!"

Most golf course deaths are caused by lightning, so it's wise to leave the course and seek safe shelter at the first grumble of thunder or the first flash of electricity in the sky. Almost all courses have a horn to warn players of dangerous weather conditions. If you hear that horn, get off the course or into safe shelter as quickly as you can. You're standing out in an open area with a metal club swinging up over your head: a lightning rod, in other words. Don't risk it.

THREE

THOU SHALT PLAY AT A GOOD PACE

The one etiquette issue golfers complain about more than any other is slow play. That's why we put a turtle on the cover of this book.

Holding up other players has less to do with skill than with awareness. Some very good golfers have been known to play too slowly (especially if money is involved), and some aware beginners and high-handicappers play at a brisk pace. There's no need to rush; just don't dawdle.

Part of the problem comes from watching the touring pros, who sometimes take eight practice swings and are known to spend two full minutes looking over a putt or waiting for a rule decision. Don't do that! They're playing for a million bucks; most likely you're not. If you bring a beginner to the course, try to play in the last group, late in the afternoon, and even then be aware that you might be holding up a group or an individual golfer who showed up late and teed off behind you. One good strategy is to let the novice golfer start out by hitting putts on the green, then move on to chip shots and putts, and then to playing the last 100 yards of the hole. Only gradually let him or her play the full-length hole, or the entire course.

When it's your turn to hit—be ready. Know what club you're going to use (this gets easier with time), and have it out of your bag and in your hand. Maybe make one practice swing, then stand over the ball, focus for a second or two, and play.

On the greens, you can size up your putt while others are putting (the one farthest from the hole always putts first, and either continues until the ball is in the hole, or says, "I'll wait", marks the ball by placing a coin or ball-marker directly behind it, then lifts up the ball and holds it until it's his turn to putt again. If you're still "away", i.e., farthest away from the hole, after your first putt, you must keep putting.) If you stand over every putt for thirty seconds before hitting it, your playing partners won't want to have you in their group again and you'll get some dirty looks in the clubhouse after the round.

The rule for a lost ball is that you have five minutes to look for it, and then you must declare it lost and take the penalty (see the rules appendix). But if those five minutes mean you're holding up the group behind you, or if you're just slower than they are (for example, if you're in a foursome and there's a single behind you, or if you're walking and the group behind you is in carts, or if you're shooting ten on most holes and they're playing to par) it's common golf courtesy to let them through, or pick up your ball and walk to the next hole. After you wave them forward, make sure to get out of their way—stand safely behind a tree if you can— but let them play through.

If you're fairly certain you won't find the ball you just hit, take one quick look and move on. If you hit a ball out of bounds—i.e., beyond the line of white stakes or off the course entirely—or if you lose a ball in the trees, then you have to hit another from the original position and take a one-stroke penalty. This is called a "stroke and distance" penalty. So, for example, if you've hit your tee shot out of bounds, you have to hit again from the tee and that is your third shot (two swings plus the penalty stroke).

On those occasions when you're not 100% sure the ball is "O.B." or lost, to avoid having to walk all the way back and start over again, you should hit what's called a "provisional" ball. Tell your playing partners, "I'm hitting a provisional. That first one was a Titleist, this one's a Calloway." Or "That first one was a Srixon 4, this one is a Srixon 2" (each sleeve of balls is numbered). You then hit the provisional from the same spot where you hit the ball you think is lost. If this happens with your tee ball, you should wait until your playing partners have hit their first ball before you hit your second. When you get up to the place where the ball disappeared, you either play the original ball—if you find it and it's in bounds—or you play your provisional with the "stroke and distance" penalty.

The penalty for losing a ball in a lateral hazard— usually a wet or swampy place, sometimes thick woods or an environmentally protected area—always marked by red stakes—is stroke but not distance. That is, you drop a ball there –not where you hit from—and take a one shot penalty. (See the rules appendix for how and where to take a drop.) If the stakes are yellow—a regular water hazard, not a lateral one—then you have to drop behind the yellow stakes, i.e., farther from the hole, not beside it.

It's not a bad idea to carry an extra ball in your pocket, so that, if you do hit a shot into a water hazard or out of bounds you don't have to go back to your bag to fetch another one. This second ball should not have the identical make and number of the first ball.

Try to develop the habit of looking behind you on the course every few minutes, no matter how excited you are about your game and how well or poorly you're playing. Be aware of the people in the group behind you because if you're very slow and inconsiderate, you're making them—and all the groups behind them on the course—absolutely miserable.

If someone does let you or your group go through, play quickly but without hurry (rushing will lead to poor shots and just slow you down again) and remember to offer them a "Thank you, have a great day," or some similar acknowledgement of their courtesy.

Every golf course is set up with two or more sets of tee boxes, sometimes as many as five. They're usually different colors—red, white, blue, black, gold, or something similar. Often, red tees are the "front" tees. Beginners, and those who don't hit the ball very far should play from those most forward tees. As you improve, you can move back a set or two, but only the very best players ordinarily tee off from the "tips"—the tee box farthest from the green.

Either when you call the course or show up in person, the employee behind the desk at the pro shop will assign you a tee time. Don't be late! It's fine to hit some balls on the practice range, or stroke a few putts on the practice green (on many courses you aren't allowed to chip onto a practice green—there will usually be a sign saying this, and sometimes a separate area for practicing your chipping and sand shots) but if you have a 10:18 tee time, you and the other members of your group should be at the tee and ready to go by 10:10.

FOUR

THOU SHALT RESPECT THE COURSE

Remember: on any given day, there might be a hundred or more players coming along behind you, so, in addition to playing at a good pace, please treat the course kindly. Here are some suggestions:

After hitting out of a bunker (sometimes also called a "sand trap"), take a few seconds to rake it smooth—erase your footprints, the mark made by your club's contact with the sand, and the mark where your ball landed and rolled (It's an act of kindness to occasionally rake even the footprints of less considerate golfers who preceded you.) Some courses will ask you to leave the rake in the bunker after you use it; others will ask you to set it down beside the bunker. If you walk up onto a green after leaving a sand trap, take a second to tap the sand from the bottoms of your shoes so it does

not get on the green and obstruct a future player's putt. It's always best to walk into and out of a bunker from the low end so you disturb less sand.

If you take a divot on the fairway or tee box, either fetch the scrap of turf, replace it, and tamp it down with your foot, or—and many clubs prefer this— use the divot mix most courses provide in a plastic bottle on your cart and sprinkle some on the bare dirt so the grass there will quickly grow back.

The greens are the most vulnerable part of a golf course. Walk softly. Never run or jump on a green.

Never bring your bag or golf cart onto or even very close to the green. Don't swivel your feet so your spikes (even the plastic ones) make marks. Don't lean on your putter so it makes a dent, and never toss your putter up in the air so that it falls and dents the green. If you've hit an approach shot from a good distance away and your ball has landed hard on the putting surface and made a mark, use your divot tool (you should always carry one) to properly repair it (push the tines of the tool in around the perimeter of the mark, push the top end of the tines gently toward the center after each

thrust downward, then tap down the repaired mark with your putter. It won't look perfect, but it will be smooth enough to give any players behind you a fair chance, and the grass will soon grow back.)

Don't leave your cigarette butts, candy wrappers, soda or beer cans for someone else to pick up. There are almost always trash bins on the tee; if you don't see any, store the trash in your bag or cart until you finish the last hole. And tap your cigar ashes somewhere off the putting surface.

FIVE

Thou Shalt Be A Good Driver

If you use a gas or electric cart on the golf course, pay attention to the rules of the road. On some days—or every day on some courses—you'll see a sign saying "Cart Path Only" or "Cart Path Only On This Hole". Sometimes the course starter (who sends you off on the first tee), or the person who checks you in at the golf shop will inform you of this. "Cart Path Only" means you should not drive the cart off the path, even to park it. Usually this rule comes into play on days after a rain where a cart can make deep tire tracks in the turf and cause serious damage. Some courses will have signs saying "Ninety-Degree Rule", which means you keep the cart off the fairway until you reach your ball, then you turn at a ninety-degree angle and go to your ball. This minimizes the cart traffic on the fairway turf.

Sometimes you'll see a sign that says "Scatter" at the point where carts leave a paved path. This means try to take a little different route off the path to save the turf there.

Golf carts tip over much more easily than cars do, so be extremely careful on even moderately sloped land. Excessive speed, or turning too quickly increases the chances of a flip.

Don't lean out of a cart when it's moving, and don't hang an arm or leg out there either.

Never drive drunk or buzzed—even on an empty golf course.

Most courses have a minimum age requirement for drivers of carts, or ask that all drivers be licensed for the real road.

Some courses will provide a "handicap flag" for carts used by people who have difficulty walking or other physical limitations. These carts are allowed to drive closer to the green, but never on it or on the apron.

If you're approaching the next tee and see that players there are getting ready to hit their drives, keep the cart at some distance to them and keep the engine as quiet as you can.

Never drive a cart close to a green or a sand trap (unless you have a handicap flag). There are usually small signs on the fairway saying "Carts" with an arrow pointing right or left. Don't go past these signs in the direction of the green unless you move off to the side the arrow indicates.

Don't drive your cart into the woods. Park and walk; it will be good for the waistline and keep you from getting stuck, damaging the cart, or injuring your rider with a low branch snapping into her face.

SIX

THOU SHALT BE COURTEOUS

Almost all courses have some kind of dress code. This usually requires a shirt with a collar and usually prohibits jeans, cargo shorts and short-shorts, tank tops, shoes with heels, and T-shirts. Neat shorts are acceptable almost everywhere. Some people prefer sneakers to golf shoes—which is fine—but most courses now prohibit the old-fashioned golf shoes with metal spikes. A few very snobby places won't let you wear your golf hat facing backwards in the "rally cap" position.

Some other suggestions for good manners on the course:

If your playing partner brought a wedge and a putter up onto the green—this happens often and is perfectly fine—pick up her wedge and hand it to her after she holes out her putt. Volunteer to lift the pin out of

the hole if you are closest to the hole and have the shortest first putt in your group. Lay it down gently, far from other players' lines of putting. Or if you hole out first, pick up the flag and be ready to replace it when all players are finished. If there's a brisk wind, hold the pin so the flag doesn't snap and make noise. A player always has the right to ask that the flag be removed, even if his ball is off the putting surface. But if your ball is on the green, you must take the flag out or have it "tended" before putting. In the case of long putts, your playing partner may ask you to "tend" the flag, that is, to lift it out of its place but keep the base of the flag in the hole so the person putting can see the target. Once the ball is struck, the attending player lifts the flag out and moves away.

Try not to walk or step in someone else's putting line; if you do so accidentally, apologize. It's a good practice to mark your ball on the green if it's not your turn to putt. It is legal for a player to ask you to move your marker if it's in or near his putting line. He'll say something like, "Can you move it one to the right, please?" The correct way to do this is to place your putter head on the green so that the tip or heel is next to the ball mark and the putter points to something nearby—a tree, usually. Keeping the putter head on the green, pick up your marker and place it at the other end the putter, i.e., the length of one putter-head away. Remember to place your marker back in the original spot before you putt, using the same technique (in tournaments there is a penalty if you forget). It's good manners, after you've putted out, to remind your fellow player to replace his marker if you have asked him to move it.

After you put down your marker (always just behind the ball) and lift your ball from the green, it's legal
to clean it of mud or grass—most players carry a towel
attached to their bag for this purpose. Another player
can ask you to mark and move your ball when it's in
her line, even if it's not on the putting surface, but if
your ball isn't on the green, you cannot clean the ball
before replacing it.

Also:

Watch closely when your partners are hitting and pay attention to where their balls land—especially if their shots bounce off the fairway.

Help your playing partners look for a lost ball as if it's your own ball you're searching for.

If you look for a few minutes and don't find your own lost ball, don't keep your friends tramping around in the trees endlessly. Say, "Thanks, let's move on," and either hit your provisional ball (as explained earlier) or take a drop and a penalty according to the rules of golf.

It's perfectly fine to fish for lost balls—your own or others—in a water hazard, but not if there are people waiting behind you.

After the first hole, the golfer with the lowest score on the previous hole has "the honors", that is, he or she gets to tee off first. If you are playing from different sets of tees, the person using the tees farthest from the hole generally has the honors, no matter his score on the previous hole.

Try not to trash talk unless it's something your friends like and engage in. If someone hits a terrible shot or is having a terrible day, the best option is a respectful silence. Occasionally you can say something like, "We've all been there," or "I know how it feels, believe me," but tread gently.

Unless you are a great player, a teacher, or you're playing with a child or an absolute beginner, it's wise not to offer advice. This is especially true with a spouse who's learning the game, or with someone you're dating or hoping to date. Let the pros do the teaching, in a paid lesson. The only exception is when a player asks for help, as in, "Can you see what I'm doing wrong, Millie?"

Be generous with compliments, praise, and encouragement, but don't overdo. Don't say "Great shot, Evelyn!" when you know she wanted something better, or when the shot is mediocre by her standards.

See Commandment #1 regarding silence, and Commandment #3 regarding pace of play.

Try not to let your shadow fall across someone else's putting line when he's lining up his putt or making his stroke on the green. This is more difficult late in the day when shadows are long.

If you are a single, or part of a twosome or threesome and a stranger asks to join up with you on the first tee, it's usually polite to welcome him or her into your group. Some courses will require this. You can do this at any point on the course, too.

On the first tee, tell your playing partners what brand of ball you're playing, and use a permanent marker to mark the ball in such a way that you and your playing partners can see it belongs to you. This comes in handy if two balls are hit close to each other on a fairway (plus, there is a penalty for hitting the wrong ball.) or if your ball ends up half-buried in leaves and you have to identify it.

Unless the course is extremely quiet—say, at the end of the season or in terrible weather— never play in a group larger than four. Most courses won't allow this in any case.

SEVEN

THOU SHALT MANAGE YOUR MOOD

If you're having the day from hell on the course, try to limit your cursing, muttering, and negativity as much as humanly possible. Your playing partner might be having the day from heaven, or, at least, might want to enjoy the round.

Never, under any circumstances, throw a golf club, no matter what you see some pros do on TV.

Never damage the course in anger (or not in anger). Don't slam your club into the ground or gouge out an extra divot, and don't bang your putter down on a green.

These guidelines for good behavior not only contribute to the enjoyment of your playing partners, but will ultimately make you enjoy the game more and likely play better. If you hit a bad shot, make one comment, then shake it off. If you're having an awful day,

27

try to laugh at yourself, and remember: you are not starving, not in jail, not being tortured, and not at work.

EIGHT

THOU SHALT BE GENEROUS

If you can, buy a little something from the person on the food cart. She—and it's almost always a she—isn't getting rich, and is driving around out there in the heat or cold or rain trying to make your day more pleasant. Let her know clearly with hand gestures or words that you do or do not want her to stop. Flirt if you must, but keep offensive remarks to yourself. Tip her—and the people who set your bag up at the bag drop (where you leave your bag when you drive up in your car)—as generously as you can. Thank or compliment the people you see working on the grounds crew, or at least acknowledge their humanity with a wave or a nod.

If you play for money and lose, pay up immediately even if you owe the winner fifty cents and she's a billionaire. Few things are worse than a golfer who loses a bet and then conveniently forgets to pay up.

Treat your friends to lunch once in a while after a round, or spring for the cost of drinks or chips or a burger at the turn or from the food cart.

Buy a bag of balls for the range and share it, or leave some for the next person to use—even if you do not know that person.

If you make a hole-in-one, buy a drink for everyone in the bar after your round. This can be expensive, but it doesn't happen often, and it's one of the game's great old traditions.

NINE

Thou Shalt Learn The Rules

The Rules of Golf (published in booklet form by the United States Golf Association—a good organization, which you can join for $25 a year) can be purchased for a small fee at most pro shops. The rules are fairly elaborate and in some cases complicated, but in almost all situations a basic understanding of a few rules will suffice: How to properly take a drop. What constitutes a hazard and what you can and cannot do there. How and when to take penalty strokes, etc. (See the rules appendix of this book for a list of the most commonly encountered rules, and brief explanations.)

Unless you're out alone and just fooling around, or unless your playing partners agree that you will all bend the rules (that you'll "pick up" short putts, for one common example, rather than having to hole them out;

that you can take a mulligan after a bad shot, or a "breakfast ball" on the first swing of the day if you don't like your opening drive) then you should know the rules and abide by them. If your playing partners are going by the official rules, it's rude to say "I'll just hit another one" after a bad shot. It's also not legal to "improve your lie" on the fairway, though you will see a fair number of people who do this. Play it as it lies: it will ultimately help your game.

Most teachers, coaches, and good golfers agree that playing by the rules will make you a better golfer in the long run, so avoiding mulligans, taking fair drops, and holing out even your one-foot putts will help you— especially if you plan to play in tournaments, where these rules will always be enforced.

TEN

THOU SHALT NOT CHEAT

Golf is a game of honorable men and women. Some groups will agree, as noted above, to play by their own set of rules, allowing mulligans, "gimmes" on short putts, creative scorekeeping, improved lies, etc. That's fine.

But cheating is inexcusable. Putting down a five in competition when you know you made a six, taking a drop closer to the hole after hitting into a hazard, grounding your club in a sand trap or hazard without taking the penalty, "adjusting" your lie in the fairway, "improving" your lie in the woods, putting false scores into the computer that calculates your handicap, and so on—these things are a species of dishonesty that often extends into more important parts of life.

After you've been playing for a while, you can start "entering" your scores after every round. Most courses have a computer in the clubhouse for this purpose. You enter your score and the course slope and rating (these numbers are a measure of the course's difficulty from various tees, and they are usually found on the score card; often you only have to enter the course name and the tees you played from and the computer will register the proper slope and rating), and the computer calculates your handicap—which is based on the best ten of your twenty most recent scores. Many people avoid having a handicap altogether, which is perfectly okay. But if you ever plan to play in a tournament, a handicap is essential, and can give you a chance to win prizes or money, even against better players. Tournaments almost always have a "gross" and a "net" winner. The "net" score is your actual score minus your handicap. Some tournaments are played at full handicap, some at 90% or 75% of handicap, etc. Having a handicap also gives you an absolutely accurate measure of how good you are.

Golf is the only sport in which players call penalties on themselves—even at the top level, where the extra stroke can mean the loss of many thousands of dollars or a prestigious tournament. Playing by the rules—however strictly or loosely you and your friends interpret them—is part of the beauty of the game and really a measure of your character. Respect yourself and your fellow golfers. Don't cheat.

COMMANDMENT 10A

THOU SHALT HAVE FUN

Golf can be absolutely maddening, at all levels, but especially when you first start out. It's a tremendously difficult sport, and it can be years before you learn to play with some proficiency (lessons, instructional books and videos, and lots of time at the driving range and practice green can help). But it's a beautiful activity— you're outdoors, facing a great mental and physical challenge; you can play until you're 100; you'll meet some good people, and find courses almost anywhere in the world. So here is the most important rule: enjoy the game!

APPENDIX A

SOME BASIC RULES

As mentioned, the complete rules of golf are detailed and complicated. They can be purchased in a small-format booklet at most courses. However, the rules listed below will cover you in 90% of the situations you are likely to face on a course. In tournaments, these rules will always be enforced. In casual play, most players decide within their group how strictly they will obey the rules.

1. Fourteen clubs is the maximum allowed. You can have any combination of clubs you like, and you can carry less if you like. A ball retriever is not counted as a club. Perhaps for superstitious reasons, good players rarely carry one.

2. White stakes mark out-of-bounds. As mentioned above, if you hit your ball out of bounds, you must take

a one-stroke penalty and play again from the place where you hit your errant shot, even if that means going all the way back to the tee. For example, if you hit out of bounds on your second shot, you are now hitting four (your third swing, plus one penalty stroke).

3. Yellow stakes mark a water hazard: if you hit into this hazard you have to drop your ball on the side of the hazard from which you hit, not on the green side. Red stakes mark what's called a lateral hazard. If you hit into a lateral hazard you have four options: 1) you may play the ball if you can (i.e., if it's not under ten feet of water; you can do this in a regular hazard, too) but you cannot "ground" your club before you hit the ball. That is, you cannot first set it down on the water, grass, or ground before you swing. 2) you may drop a ball up to two club lengths from the point where the ball last crossed the red hazard line, though this cannot be closer to the hole. Or you can drop at a point on the opposite margin of the water hazard, equidistant from the hole. 3) you can draw an imaginary line from the point where your ball last crossed the hazard line to the pin and go back along that line as far as you want and drop a ball there. 4) you may go back to where you struck the last shot and drop there. With the exception of #1, all these options require a one-stroke penalty.

4. You may not leave the pin in the hole while putting unless it is tended by another player (who will lift it as the ball approaches), or your ball is off the putting surface when you strike it.

5. For the first shot on every hole, you can choose to set your ball up on a small wooden or plastic tee, or not (most people do, but on some short holes—par-threes— some players prefer to hit from the turf.) On the fairway and in the rough you must play your ball as it lies.

6. If your ball comes to rest on a cart track, or if you must stand on the track in order to hit your ball in the normal fashion, find the nearest "point of relief" where you are not standing on the track and your ball is not on it. From that point, you can drop your ball within one club length, but no closer to the hole. No penalty.

7. To drop the ball correctly, hold your arm straight out sideways at shoulder height and release the ball. If it bounces closer to the hole, or moves more than two club lengths or back into a hazard, drop it a second time. If the same thing happens a second time (this often occurs if you are on a slope), then you may place the ball on the spot where it hit the ground on that second drop.

8. In wet conditions some courses will allow a "lift, clean, and place rule" which means that you can mark your ball (only on the fairway), pick it up, clean off the mud, and set it back roughly in the same place with no penalty.

9. If your ball is partly or fully embedded in soft earth (except in a sand trap) you can always lift, clean, and place it. No penalty.

10. If your ball is in "casual water", that is, a puddle or wet ground that is not part of an actual water hazard, you may take a free lift, clean it, and drop it on the nearest dry ground no closer to the hole. No penalty.

11. You must take a penalty stroke if you move twigs, stones, or other objects from around your ball and the ball moves.

12. You take a penalty stroke if you make a practice swing under a tree and you knock down a branch or even a leaf. A very picky rule, so be careful.

13. There is a two-stroke penalty for hitting the wrong ball.

14. On the scorecard, most courses will print their "local rules". An example might be: Take a free lift from the flower beds on hole #9. If there is a white line drawn around a patch of ground (not a white line signifying Out of Bounds), this signifies "ground under repair" and you may lift your ball and drop it no closer to the hole without penalty.

15. You can take relief—i.e. a free drop—from man-made objects like 150-yard markers (usually small posts with black and white bands on it; the 100-yard markers are usually red, and the 200 yard markers blue), electric boxes, and drinking fountains. But if your ball lies close to or against the fence that marks the boundary of the course, you either have to play it as it lies or move it and take a penalty.

16. At any time you can "take an unplayable lie", pick up your ball and drop it two club lengths away—no closer to the hole—with a one-stroke penalty. Or you may go back as far as you want along a line extending from the hole to the place where your shot came to rest. Also one-stroke penalty. For example, if you're in the trees and against a root, or a rock that can't be moved, or you find your ball in a bush, it's often better to take an "unplayable" than try to make an impossible

shot and only get yourself deeper into trouble. (This rule does not apply for holes made by animals—free drop there.) You third option is to take an unplayable and go back and hit from the original spot, with penalty.

17. A lost ball is played like an out-of-bounds shot: return to the place where you hit the ball and take a one-stroke penalty. (Or play your provisional. You can keep hitting the provisional with no penalty until you reach the place where your first shot disappeared. If you then find the original ball in-bounds, you can play that ball without penalty. If not, you play the provisional and add one stroke to the number of swings you have made.)

18. Sometimes—usually when chipping— you will make contact with the ball twice on the same swing. One stroke penalty.

19. If you hit the ball and it hits you (in a sand trap with a high face, for instance), two stroke penalty.

20. If you completely miss the ball, that counts as a stroke.

21. If your ball hits another player, or the caddie, bag, or equipment of another player, no penalty.

22. If you hit a ball onto the green and it knocks into a ball already there, no problem: keep your ball where it is. The other player must put his ball back to where it was—or as close as he can estimate—with no penalty to either player.

23. You get a "free lift" from cart paths and sprinkler heads, and may take a drop... but no closer to the hole.

24. If your club touches the sand, or if it touches the ground in a hazard before you make your swing, one-stroke penalty. In a sand bunker, you must hover your club near the ball when you address it. But larger bunkers that stretch alongside the fairways are sometimes called "waste bunkers" and you may ground your clubs in them with no penalty.

25. On the green, you can repair ball marks that are in your putting line, but you cannot repair marks made by a player's shoes—"spike marks". You can always remove loose impediments from your putting line, but you can't pull anything out of the ground. And you cannot straddle the line of the putt; you must have both feet on one side of the extension of that line.

26. For the first stroke of each hole, you must set your ball behind the line made by the two markers on the tee box—not in front of that line, and not to the outside of either marker.

27. On the fairway, you must play your ball as it lies, even if it lies in a divot hole made by another player.

28. Some courses will have "drop zones" on holes with water hazards. If you hit into the hazard you have the option of dropping your ball in one of these marked zones. One stroke penalty.

APPENDIX B

GOLF TERMS

<u>Stroke play</u>—competition in which the lower score wins.

<u>Match play</u>—competition in which the winner is the player who has the lower score on the most holes.

<u>Par-three, par-four, par-five</u>—short, middle-length, and longer holes.

<u>A Lay-up</u>—purposely hitting your ball a shorter distance to avoid going into a hazard.

<u>Gimme</u>—allowing another player to pick up his or her ball rather than hitting a short putt into the hole. You still count the one stroke, but you assume it will be only one.

<u>Mulligan or Breakfast Ball</u>—taking another shot without counting the penalty after hitting a bad one. Breakfast ball is a mulligan on the first swing of the day.

<u>Hook</u>—a ball that curves sharply to the left for a right-handed player (or sharply right for a left-handed player).

<u>Slice</u>—the opposite of a hook.

<u>Draw</u>—a gentle hook.

Fade—a gentle slice.

Duff—slang term for a bad shot that doesn't go far.

Blading it—hitting the ball too far, usually near the green, because the bottom edge of your club struck the middle, not the bottom of the ball.

Push—hitting the ball directly right (for right-handed players) of your target with no curve.

Yank or Pull—hitting the ball directly left (for right-handed players) of your target with no curve.

Pin, Flag, Stick, Flagstick—all names for the thin stick that fits into the hole on one end and holds the flag on the other.

Double-breaker—a putt that moves in two directions before reaching the hole.

Slider—a short left-to-right putt for a right-handed player.

Hook putt—the opposite of a slider.

Flex—the amount of flex in the shaft of your clubs. Generally speaking, players with slower swing speeds will want more flexible shafts.

Hitting it Fat—hitting the ground behind the ball so that the shot doesn't go as far as it should. Also called "laying the sod over the ball" or "chunking" it.

Hitting it Thin—the opposite of hitting it fat; topping the ball.

Ace—a hole-in-one.

<u>Eagle</u>—getting the ball into the hole in two strokes fewer than par. (An "albatross" is one stroke better than an eagle, i.e. a 2 on a par 5. Extremely rare, even at the highest levels of golf.)

<u>Birdie</u>—getting the ball into the hole in one stroke less than par.

<u>Bogey</u>—one stroke more than par.

<u>Double Bogey or "Double"</u>—two strokes more than par.

<u>Snowman</u>—making an 8 on a hole.

<u>Dogleg</u>—a hole that bends left or right like the hind leg of a dog.

<u>Downhill Lie</u>—the ball is perched on a downslope.

<u>Sidehill Lie</u>—the ball is perched on the side of a hill or small slope.

<u>Two-Club Wind</u>—a strong wind that will push against the ball and make it travel "two clubs" farther or less far than it ordinarily would. For instance, if you would normally hit a seven-iron from 150 yards, and you have a "two-club" wind in your face, then you need to hit a five-iron to make the ball go the same distance. A One-Club Wind is similar, though not as strong.

<u>Inside the Leather</u>—an old term that refers to putts that are closer to the hole than the length of the grip of the club.

Handicap—the difference between the average score you make on 18 holes, and par. So, if your handicap is 10, and par for the course is 72, you have averaged 82 for the ten best scores of your last twenty rounds. Course difficulty—measured by 'Slope' and 'Rating', and shown on the golf card— can alter this calculation somewhat.

Sandbagger—a person who cheats on his handicap, especially in tournaments. This person will say he has a 25 handicap, when he actually has a 20, which will make it easier for him to win the net prize.

Shank—a horrible word some golfers refuse to speak because of superstition. Shanking the ball means hitting it so close to the hozzle of the club (the innermost end of the clubface near the base of the shaft) that it shoots off almost directly sideways. It sometimes happens that once a player starts to shank, she cannot stop, and it is THE most frustrating part of a frustrating game.

Mayor's Office/ Position A—the place you are if your ball ends up in the ideal part of the fairway.

Up-and-Down—getting the ball from just off the green into the hole in two shots.

All Square—a golf term for "tied up" or "even", most often used in match play. If you were "one up" on the seventh tee and lost the hole, you and your opponent are now "all square."

Fried Egg—a bad lie in a bunker. The ball has settled into the sand and looks like the yolk of a sunny-side-up fried egg.

Scratch Golfer—a very good player who carries a zero handicap.

Single-digit Golfer—a quite good player whose handicap is under 10.

Kick-in Birdie—a shot hit close to the hole, leaving a very short putt for birdie.

Drive for Show, Putt for Dough—a commonly heard expression that means, when playing for money, that it's usually more important to be a good putter than a long hitter.

Duffer or Hacker—someone who does not play well.

Player—the opposite of a duffer or a hacker.

Long Over the Ball—standing too long over a shot before you swing.

Lip-Out—a putt that hits the edge of the hole but does not go in.

Bomb—a very long putt that goes in the hole.

Ready Golf—not worrying about who has the honors on the tee. Whoever is ready, hits first.

The Yips—a frustrating ailment in which the golfer flinches while making a putt and starts habitually missing very short putts.

APPENDIX C

EQUIPMENT

When you arrive at the course you should have:
Golf bag and clubs— (most courses will rent clubs and bags if you do not have them, but call first to make sure).

Three-wheeled push cart (unless you rent a gas or electric cart or carry your bag).

At least two golf gloves.

Towel.

A good supply of golf balls and tees.

Divot tool for repairing ball-marks on the green.

Several coins or ball markers for marking balls on the green.

Rain gear. Hat. Umbrella. Rain gloves (used on both hands and made so they grip better when wet.)

Golf shoes (optional).

Water and snacks.

Sun screen.

Adhesive tape or band-aides, ibuprofen.

Permanent marker.

Cash for tips and snacks and to pay off lost bets.

ENJOY THE GREAT GAME OF GOLF!

ABOUT THE AUTHOR

Roland Merullo is the author of *Passion for Golf: In Pursuit of the Innermost Game, Golfing with God,* and *The Italian Summer: Golfing and Eating in Italy,* as well as sixteen other novels and books of non-fiction on various subjects.

A former Contributing Writer to *Golf World Magazine,* he has also written for *Golf Magazine, Travel and Leisure Golf, Golf Digest,* and *Links,* and has played at great courses all over the world. An admitted golf fanatic, Roland lives with his wife and daughters in Massachusetts.

He can be reached at www.rolandmerullo.com.

ABOUT THE ILLUSTRATOR

John Recco lives and works on an old farm in the rolling hills of upstate New York with his wife and two daughters. When he is not in his studio painting, John can usually be found out in the garden or tending to one of the many projects he has in different states of completion. He can be reached at www.johnrecco.com.

Passion for Golf
In Pursuit of the Innermost Game

Roland Merullo

Most avid golfers believe that there is a profound connection between the joys and challenges of golf and the joys and challenges of living — that the more devoted we are to the game, the more we learn about ourselves.

In *Passion for Golf: In Pursuit of the Innermost Game,* Roland Merullo looks carefully at those connections and at the reasons why people find themselves irresistibly attracted to golf.

Drawing on the triumphs and travails of playing partners, friends, and family members, and mixing in anecdotes from his own adventures on and off the course, Merullo explores the notion of a 'true goal of golf,' a hidden attraction that, ultimately, has more to do with deep peace and satisfaction than with the dream of playing on the PGA tour. He finds connections between fairway lessons and the mystical wisdom of Lao Tzu, Theresa of Avila, Thoreau, Jesus, Buddha, and Walt Whitman, among many others, and looks into the role of ego, anger, and silence in golf and life.

More than anything else, *Passion for Golf* is a celebration of the game, an examination of the roots of our passion for it, and a meditation on the lessons every golfer carries away from the course and into his or her life.

Publishers Weekly wrote, "For average hackers who struggle weekly to lower their scores, this slender, accessible guide offers insight into the emotional stumbling blocks that get in the way of improvement and, most importantly, enjoyment of the game... Readers who enjoyed Michael Murphy's Zen of golf classic, *Golf in the Kingdom*, should have room for this spiritual journey in their Christmas stocking."

And, *The Washington Post* stated "...Merullo provides more than enough food for thought for even the most contemplative golfer."

* Available in print and eBook formats *

NOTES